WALTER DRAGUN'S TOWN

Crafts and Trade in the Middle Ages

by Sheila Sancha

HarperCollinsPublishers

To my mother
Phyllis Neal Green

ACKNOWLEDGMENTS

I would like to thank David Roffe for introducing me to the Hundred Rolls in the first place and for supplying so much detailed information on the history of Stamford. I am also grateful to Christine Mahany, Director (Medieval) Trust for Lincolnshire Archaeology, for advice on the castle and town. Additional help was readily available from John Smith, Curator, and the staff of the Stamford Museum.

It was a pleasure to work on such rich material. The main source of reference for the buildings came from the Royal Commission on Historical Buildings' superb volume *The Town of Stamford* published by Her Majesty's Stationery Office. The Conway Library's survey on Lincoln Cathedral was taken from the Courtauld Institute Illustration Archives, Lincoln, Parts 1, 5 and 7, published by Harvey Miller, 1976 and 1978. The aerial view on pages 46–47 was based upon the Ordnance Survey series of historical maps with the permission of the Controller of Her Majesty's Stationery Office, Crown Copyright Reserved.

As with *The Luttrell Village*, I greatly appreciate the support and encouragement given by my editors Susan Dickinson and Enid Fairhead. And I also wish to thank my son-in-law, Doug Lear, for supplying the lettering.

LONDON 1987

WALTER DRAGUN'S TOWN: CRAFTS AND TRADE IN THE MIDDLE AGES

Copyright © 1987, 1989 by Sheila Sancha
First published by William Collins Sons & Co Ltd., London
Printed in Mexico. All rights reserved.
Typography by Elynn Cohen
4 5 6 7 8 9 10
First American Edition, 1989

Library of Congress Cataloging-in-Publication Data
Sancha, Sheila.
    Walter Dragun's town : crafts and trade in the Middle Ages / Sheila Sancha.
        p.   cm.
    Summary: Presents the economic and social life of a medieval town by chronicling a week's activities in the trading center of Stanford (now Stamford), England, in 1275.
    ISBN 0-690-04804-1. — ISBN 0-690-04806-8 (lib. bdg.)
    1. Stamford (England)—Commerce—History—Juvenile literature.
2. Handicraft—England—Stamford—History—Juvenile literature.
[1. Stamford (England)—History.   2. Civilization, Medieval.]
I. Title.
HF3510.S69S26 1989
307.7'6'0942588—dc19

88-34066
CIP
AC

INTRODUCTION

This book is based on three main sources of information: the town of Stanford (the present-day spelling is Stamford), situated about a hundred miles north of London; entries in the Hundred Rolls of 1275, which is a collection of documents kept in the Public Record Office; and some delightful thirteenth-century sculpted heads, mostly from nearby Lincoln Cathedral. The town supplied the archaeology; the rolled parchments gave the names of the characters and told of the events; and the drawings of the characters are based on the carved stone heads, which appear to be portraits of real people.

In early times Stanford was famous for fine pottery, but the industry declined in the thirteenth century, when inferior pottery was brought in from the surrounding villages. The town dealt with all kinds of agricultural products, wool in particular, and by the end of the thirteenth century it had become an important center of trade and industry.

Edward I returned from his Crusade and was crowned in 1274. Shortly thereafter he made a detailed survey of his realm. The king's justices traveled up and down the country with questionnaires to be answered by the men of each district, or "hundred." The questions and answers are written in the Hundred Rolls, nicknamed Ragmen Rolls from the multitude of seals that used to hang from the parchments. There were two Stanford Rolls, one recording the comments and complaints made by the twelve most important men of the town, and the other recording those of twelve lesser men. These give a lively account of the state of the town at the time of the survey. This is the reason for setting the story in the summer of 1274.

There are no illustrations in the Hundred Rolls to show what people looked like, and there is little contemporary sculpture in Stanford. In order to visualize the characters I had to look farther afield. The Conway Library's series of photographs of Lincoln Cathedral revealed an entire population of sculpted heads, and from then on it was just a question of fitting the names to the faces.

Stanford was a seigneurial town, which means it was ruled by a lord and not directly by the king. The district south of the River Weland (the present-day spelling is Welland) was founded by Edward the Elder in 918 and belonged to the Abbot of Peterborough. The walled part of the town north of the river had been ruled by barons since the middle of the twelfth century and in 1274 was in the grip of Earl John de Warenne. Inhabitants there took their complaints to the earl's court to be heard by the earl himself, or by his seneschal, Walter Dragun.

When the barons had rebelled against the king in the middle of the thirteenth century, the Abbot of Peterborough had sided with the barons, while Earl John de Warenne had spent much of his time, though not all, supporting the king. He had been given Stanford after the Battle of Evesham in 1265 as a reward for his prowess in battle, other defections having been forgiven.

Apart from these two powerful men, there were other pressure groups in the town. Although there is no direct reference to a guild in Stanford until the next century, the merchants probably formed some kind of trade association. And the chief men of the town, as listed in the Hundred Rolls, were hard at work behind the scenes.

It was Wednesday evening August 15, 1274, and three men stood chatting in St. Paul's Street, Stanford, having a last-minute business conversation before the daylight faded. They were the wool merchant, Hugh, son of Walter of Tikencot; Reginald the Dyer; and the cloth finisher and merchant Walter the Fleming, whose fine stone house stood a few yards up the road opposite the conduit, where the housewives were collecting the nightly supply of water.

Stanford was a prosperous trading center. Horses, cattle, sheep, and grain were bought and sold in the streets. But wool was the most profitable product of all. A wealthy Florentine merchant, Fulk Clarissimus, was coming to Stanford within the next few days, and he was expected to buy a large quantity of raw wool to be shipped back and processed in his own city. But the Stanford merchants, eager to promote their local weaving industry, were discussing how to persuade the foreigner to buy cloth made in their town.

GREAT NORTH ROAD

OPEN FIELDS

CONDUIT HEAD

BROAD ST

HIGH ST

ALL SAINTS' CHURCH

ST GEORGE SQUARE

ST PETER'S CHURCH

ST MARY'S CHURCH

ST MARY ST

MARKET PLACE

ST MARY'S PLACE

ST PETER'S ST

CASTLE

ST MARY'S HILL

WEST GATE

MILL

FORDS

FORD

CASTLE MEADOW

MILL POND

FRIARS OF THE SACK

ST MARTIN'S CHURCH

FORD

HIGHGATE

ST MICHAEL'S PRIORY

ST GILES' LEPER HOSPITAL

FORD

GREAT NORTH RO

HORSE PASTURE

ERMINE STREET

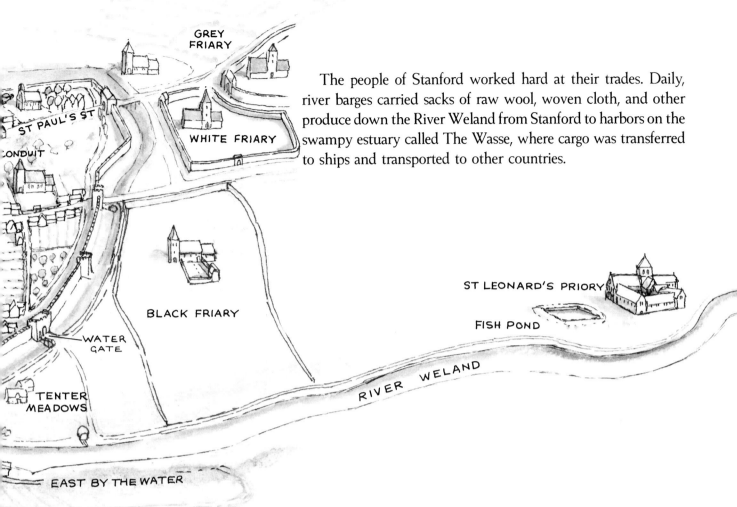

GREY FRIARY

WHITE FRIARY

ST PAUL'S ST

CONDUIT

BLACK FRIARY

WATER GATE

ST LEONARD'S PRIORY

FISH POND

RIVER WELAND

TENTER MEADOWS

EAST BY THE WATER

The people of Stanford worked hard at their trades. Daily, river barges carried sacks of raw wool, woven cloth, and other produce down the River Weland from Stanford to harbors on the swampy estuary called The Wasse, where cargo was transferred to ships and transported to other countries.

The bridge over the Weland was built around 918. But the river was not deep, and before the bridge had been built, travelers had laid stones on the riverbed and waded the shallow water. Stanford was named after one of these early stone fords.

In the ninth century a group of marauding Danes rowed upriver until they came to this important crossing place. They beached their boats and built their settlement on the north bank, in sight of Ermine Street, the ancient Roman road stretching from London to York, which eventually became known as the Great North Road.

As time passed travelers began to leave this paved road and go to Stanford to pick up goods that had arrived by river. The Great North Road branched eastward down the hill, forded two streams, and ascended to Stanford market, just outside the Danish borough. This soon became the main thoroughfare. When the bridge was built, the road shifted eastward yet again. The Great North Road is still used as a main route today.

By 1274 merchants and artisans like Walter, Hugh, and Reginald had taken best advantage of road and river, and turned the small original Danish settlement into one of the busiest towns in England.

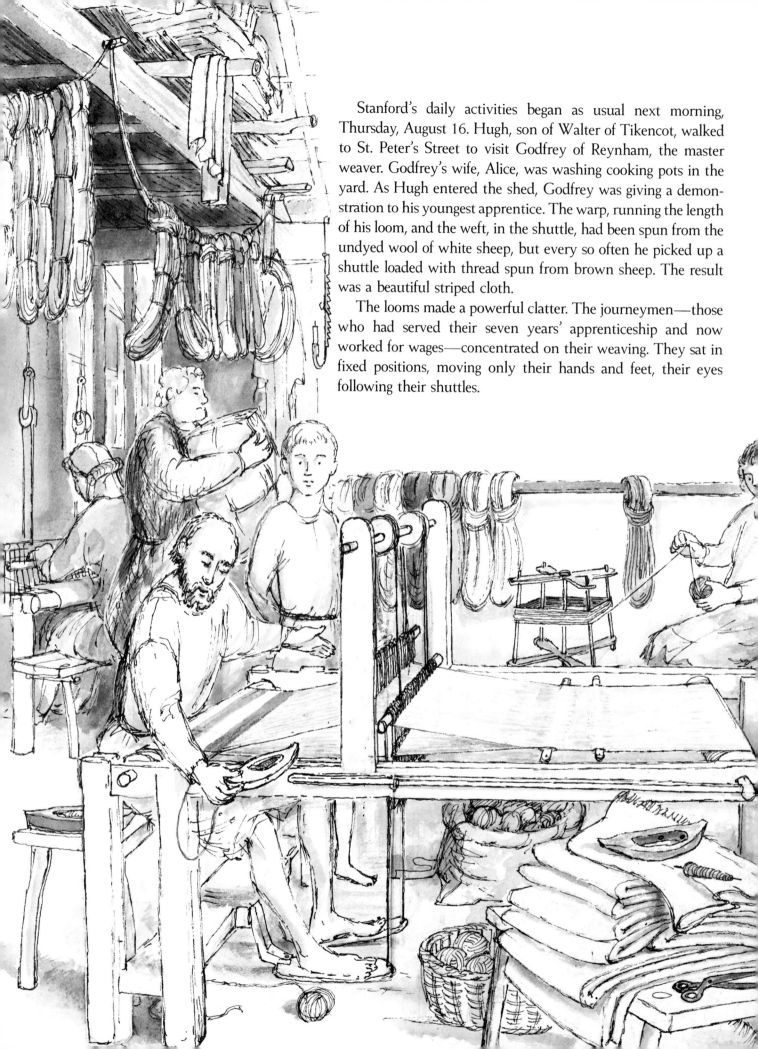

Stanford's daily activities began as usual next morning, Thursday, August 16. Hugh, son of Walter of Tikencot, walked to St. Peter's Street to visit Godfrey of Reynham, the master weaver. Godfrey's wife, Alice, was washing cooking pots in the yard. As Hugh entered the shed, Godfrey was giving a demonstration to his youngest apprentice. The warp, running the length of his loom, and the weft, in the shuttle, had been spun from the undyed wool of white sheep, but every so often he picked up a shuttle loaded with thread spun from brown sheep. The result was a beautiful striped cloth.

The looms made a powerful clatter. The journeymen—those who had served their seven years' apprenticeship and now worked for wages—concentrated on their weaving. They sat in fixed positions, moving only their hands and feet, their eyes following their shuttles.

Hugh shouted above the noise that he needed more cloth, but Godfrey yelled back he was short of spun yarn. Spinning was done by the Stanford housewives and countrywomen, but the weavers' demands always outstripped the supply, and many looms had to stand idle. Godfrey promised to send Alice and the youngest apprentice to the village of Tinewell, to see if a fresh supply of yarn was available.

Alice was delighted to be out on such a bright sunny day. She rode the donkey, and the apprentice walked. When they arrived at Tinewell, they found the village women busily sorting wool into different lengths, and combing, carding, and spinning. Long locks of wool from the fleeces were combed, as hair is combed, until all the strands hung smooth and straight. The combs were fitted with steel teeth and heated on a charcoal pot to make the work easier. Short locks, intended for a thicker type of cloth, were brushed between carding boards fitted with prickly teasel heads from the tall teasel plants in their gardens. The brushing also cleaned and straightened the fibers. Spinning was done by the age-old method of distaff and spindle.

Alice sought out Agnes, who made the best spun yarn in Tinewell, and bought all the stock she had in her house, but Alice still asked for more. Agnes explained that the work took much time and trouble. Wool from the two fleeces hanging on the fence needed sorting and washing before it was ready for her busy fingers.

The women of Tinewell did their household washing in the wide stream that flowed past their village to join the River Weland. They used flat wooden "hands" to beat the dirt out of the linen. Agnes would carry her supply of sorted wool down to the water to join the rest of the women. Short wool was put in baskets and rinsed in the running stream to wash out grime and grease. The long combing wool was twisted and wrung between two forked poles as it floated in the water. An extract of the soapwort plant, which grew along the bank, turned frothy in water and helped with the cleaning.

Having bought all the best yarn in the village, Alice and the apprentice walked the two miles back to Stanford, with the donkey almost hidden by the bulky sacks. They rested on the ridge of the hill and looked across at the town with its fine churches and houses crowded together inside the strong stone walls. Stonemasons had started building the walls in 1261, when King Henry III had given a murage grant to the inhabitants of Stanford. A murage grant gave townspeople the right to impose a tax on strangers and tradespeople entering or leaving their town, and the money collected at the gates could then be used to build a defensive wall to protect them from likely enemies. Alice could remember a time when Stanford had been defended by a timber palisade, but this had been torn down and was being replaced by the new wall and towers. Although the work had taken a long time, it was now nearing completion.

There was an angry crowd at the West Gate. The gatekeeper was demanding toll money, and someone was refusing to pay.

Tolls were paid by strangers coming in from the surrounding
towns and villages and folk traveling up the Great North Road;
but inhabitants of Stanford, like Alice, did not have to pay. As she
approached, Alice could see it was no stranger. It was Henry
Cobb, the quarryman, who lived outside the town walls but in
All Saints' parish, which was considered part of the town.

Henry Cobb had driven his load of stone roofing tiles through the gate and had come to a halt when the gatekeeper grabbed hold of the lead horse's bridle. Hotly indignant, Henry declared he had never been asked for toll money before and carried no pennies in his pocket. He tugged off his shirt and offered to leave it as a pledge while he went to discuss the matter with Walter the Fleming, who needed the tiles to replace a roof. But the gatekeeper refused the shirt, and the cart stayed where it was.

Then Walter Dragun, the most unpopular man in Stanford, walked up the street, and the crowd quickly dispersed. Walter Dragun was seneschal to Earl John de Warenne, lord of Stanford; but the earl seldom came to the town, and so his seneschal made all the necessary judgments in his absence.

Walter Dragun not only said the toll had to be paid but added a fine for Henry's surly refusal. He would impound the horses until he received the money. Reluctantly, Henry Cobb pulled on his shirt, got down from his cart, and walked off to see if he could beg a small advance payment on the tiles from Walter the Fleming. Meanwhile, Walter Dragun summoned a bailiff, Hugh Bunting, and ordered him to unhitch the horses and follow him back to the castle.

Hugh Bunting followed Walter Dragun through the dark gatehouse passage into the sunlit bailey. The horses were handed to an underbailiff, Nicholas Pot, and tethered in a shed. Walter Dragun was not only the seneschal but constable of the castle as well, and he was fully aware of his status as he walked down to the castle hall, overlooking the river. A group of bailiffs and underbailiffs waited outside the door to carry out his orders.

Although he was seldom seen, the oppressive power of Earl John de Warenne was felt by the people of Stanford each time they passed the walls of his castle.

The Normans had originally built a timber castle in 1068 on a high rocky site, west of the early Danish borough. The castle was rebuilt later with a circular stone keep. The bailey, which

sloped down to the water meadows by the river, was enclosed by stone walls and towers. River water turned the wheel of the castle corn mill, and there were fisheries in the lower mill pool. The castle first came into the hands of the Warenne family in 1205, and it had remained with them, on and off, ever since.

John de Warenne, seventh Earl of Surrey, one of the most powerful barons of England, had once fought against Henry III, the old king, but had made amends by going on Crusade in 1268. He was now loyal to the new king, Edward I. However, the earl took the law into his own hands when it suited him, and he had recently quarreled with two of his neighbors. One of them had been so violently attacked by the earl's men-at-arms that he had died of his injuries.

When an urgent problem arose, Walter Dragun would send messengers to seek out the earl, wherever he might be. The earl had many castles and other estates; but if he was not in any of these places, he was probably competing in some tournament. Fighting was his profession, and he had to keep in practice. From his seat in the saddle and fully armed, he would hear the seneschal's account of the problem as related by his messenger, consider the case, then shout his answering instructions to his clerk, who wrote them down on a parchment.

The letter was then handed to the messenger, and the
messenger rode back to Stanford to hand it to Walter Dragun,
who could not read; but he would summon his clerk, Walter
Black, to read the message for him.

In his decision to fine Henry Cobb, though, Walter Dragun
needed no consultation with the earl. Unfair or not, the fine
would have to be paid.

After helping Henry out of his predicament with a small advance payment on the roofing tiles, Walter the Fleming walked down to check the cloth in his fulling shed by the river.

Cloth woven from combed wool was sold in rolls of standard width straight from the weavers' looms; but cloth from carded wool often underwent the additional processes of fulling and tenting. The cold and the wind came through the weave of untreated cloth, and the fulling process blocked the minute gaps between the threads. The grease was removed from the cloth by soaking it in a mixture of fuller's earth (a kind of clay) and water. Then, in many cases, the cloth was trampled by the bare feet of men and boys until the wool was shrunk and matted and the warp and weft indistinguishable. (Fullers were often called walkers.) But most of Walter the Fleming's cloth was fulled in his mill, where the water-driven wheel operated gigantic hammers, and the cloth was beaten mechanically.

The fulled cloth came out of the water twice as thick as before, but far less than the original length and width. One selvage edge of the cloth was then hooked to the top rail of a tenting frame, and the other selvage edge fixed to the hooks of a heavy beam that hung below and pulled the cloth back into shape as it dried in the open air. Returned to the workshed, the tented cloth was beaten with thistle heads fixed in wooden frames until the surface of the material was covered with fluff. Skilled shearmen clipped off the ragged fluff with gigantic shears, and the cloth was then ready to show to Walter the Fleming, who checked it for quality, weight, length, and width. Only the best material would be good enough to show to Fulk Clarissimus, the Florentine merchant: Walter's reputation was at stake.

At week's end, Reginald the Dyer sat in his countinghouse, counting his money. The weekly accounts took all of Saturday morning because he was rich and the currency was in little silver pennies. The coins were dirty and old: some were bent, and slivers of silver had been clipped from others until they were no longer circular. People melted the clippings to make a bit of profit on the side. Reginald arranged the coins in neat piles: twelve pennies to one shilling, and twenty shillings to a pound; but these were only sums for reckoning—there were no coins for shillings or pounds. Reginald's father remembered a time when the king had introduced a gold coin, but it had complicated, not simplified, matters, and had been withdrawn in 1257. Foreign merchants brought in gold and silver coins from their countries; the coins were turned into English currency by the money changers down at the docks.

Having locked his silver pennies in a chest, Reginald hurried from his house to the Water Gate, then out of the town to his dye house by the river. Steam hung around the beams of the shed, and men worked with stained hands as they heaved the heavy cloth from the dye vats, squeezing out the water. They also dyed the raw wool, or dipped the skeins of spun yarn in and out of the vats. Reginald the Dyer did not waste time on country dyes: red earth oxides, which the shepherds used for marking their sheep; yellows from the scrapings of the beekeepers' hives; greens from plants and lichens; green-grays from wood ash; or the purple-blue of autumn blackberries. He traded for the nobility and used extremely expensive imported dyes: red kermes made of tiny dried insects from Spain; yellow saffron from stamens of crocuses growing in India; imperial purple extracted from glands in millions of Mediterranean shellfish. The list was endless. Reginald was proud of his brilliant range of wools, skeins, and cloth: the best on the market.

However hard the townspeople worked, they never produced enough to satisfy the merchants. But all tools were laid aside on Sundays, when the people crowded into their parish churches to pray for success in the coming week. Sunday, August 19, was a historic day, a day to be remembered. When King Henry III died in 1272, his son, Edward, was away on Crusade. But a messenger had just arrived in Stanford to announce that Edward was back in England and at this very moment was being crowned in Westminster Abbey with his queen, Eleanor of Castile. The priest of All Saints' in the Market delivered a special sermon to wish King Edward I a peaceful and prosperous reign.

All Saints' in the Market was the finest church in Stanford and had been standing for forty years, although there had been an earlier church on the site. Pictures from the Old and New Testaments decorated the walls; figures of kings and saints glowed when the sun shone through the colored window glass; and the nave was dominated by a huge wooden statue of Christ on the Cross, behind which the boards filling the chancel arch were painted with life-sized figures of the Virgin Mary, St. Mary Magdalene, and St. Peter. The congregation stood or sat around the walls and on the floor as they stared at the paintings and pondered the Bible stories.

Having finished his sermon on this special day, the priest now celebrated Mass, assisted by his deacon.

About a quarter of the population of Stanford was in Holy Orders of one sort or another. There were the black-robed Benedictine monks of St. Leonard's Priory a short distance east of the town, which belonged to the great monastery of Durham. Boys were sent to St. Leonard's to be educated before going to Durham to become monks. St. Michael's Priory, a house of Benedictine nuns, was owned by the Abbot of Burg and built on sloping ground overlooking castle meadow, south of the river.

Unlike the monks and nuns, who were shut away behind high walls, the friars mixed freely with the townspeople. There were Black Friars, White Friars, and Grey Friars, whose friaries were east of the town wall, and the four Friars of the Sack, whose house was outside the West Gate.

Parish priests, who lived separately in their priests' houses, looked after the spiritual welfare of their parishioners and held the services in their churches, while the friars preached either from the shelter of their own churches, just outside the town walls, or in the streets and marketplaces.

Friars were immensely popular, and it was the Grey Friars who had built the conduits in St. Paul's Street and the High Street for the good of the community, although the merchants had given them the money. Water flowed from a natural spring just north of the town and descended through wooden gutters and lead pipes to fill the tanks in the conduits, so water was available whenever anyone pulled up the pegs in the spouts. On this coronation Sunday the Grey Friars had cut off the water supply and filled the High Street conduit with wine!

The thirty-three nuns of St. Michael celebrated the coronation of their king in their own special way, enjoying an extra pittance of fruit, nuts, and wine, which they ate in silence with their midday meal. They prayed to the Glory of God at least seven times each day. Unless they were ill, they never had a full night's sleep, because matins took place before two o'clock in the morning, when the subprioress rang a little bell in the dorter, woke up the nuns, and with a sharp tap of her cane, reprimanded anyone who refused to get up. When dressed, the nuns all trooped down the night stairs to the church and took their places in the choir stalls, while their sacristan lit the candles and lamps and rang the great bell in the tower. There were also a prior and priests to take the services.

Few citizens of Stanford could read or write and, in general, the only educated people were in Holy Orders. Ordinary folk spoke an early form of English, clerics communicated in Latin, and the nobility conversed in French. At the church song schools, choirboys learned the words and meanings of their songs. Ambitious young men were educated for the priesthood under the direction of the church in neighboring cathedral cities, and those from rich families, or with patrons, studied at the universities of Oxford or Cambridge. Monasteries had their own schools, and occasionally a wealthy benefactor would found an academic hall.

One such benefactor, Sir Robert Luterel (father of Sir Geoffrey Luttrell, who commissioned *The Luttrell Psalter*), held his main estate some twenty miles away at Gerneham, and among other properties, he had a town house in St. Peter's Street, Stanford. This house was promised to the Abbey of Sempringham, in the neighborhood of Gerneham, for use as an academic hall; but the property was not transferred until 1301. Meanwhile the Sempringham scholars were educated in another house, to be beaten with the birch if they failed in their lessons of Latin grammar, rhetoric, and dialectic. Rhetoric taught them how to speak eloquently; dialectic taught them how to argue.

For the townspeople, the Monday after coronation Sunday was like any other Monday. It was market day. Traders set up their stalls and loaded them with goods brought in from the surrounding villages. The best sites were in Broad Street, St. Mary's Place, St. George's Square, and outside All Saints' Church, which was the main marketplace overlooking the castle gatehouse.

Hugh Bunting, the bailiff, and the underbailiff, Nicholas Pot, came up from the gatehouse to inspect the goods and found fault with everything. They sniffed the fish and pinched the crusty new bread. Then Hugh Bunting approached Henry of Cottesmore, the tanner, and accused him of overcharging for his leather. This was totally unjust. Henry was a conscientious worker, and the hides were well worth the money. Having picked out the best calfskin, Hugh confiscated it as a fine, tucking it under his belt. Then he noticed noisy laughter coming from the stall behind him. Thomas Savage was buying new clothes for himself with the help of some friends. Hugh Bunting, reminded of another trick Walter Dragun had taught him for extorting money from the townspeople, suddenly swung around and accused Thomas Savage of harboring robbers in his house. Thomas was dumbfounded and then fiercely denied the charge; but Hugh only called Nicholas Pot and John Gerneys, a big burly fellow who happened to be with him, and after a short scuffle, Thomas Savage was marched away to the castle prison.

Henry of Cottesmore went to work the next day in an ugly mood, thinking of his confiscated property. He had spent many days on that calfskin. It had been soaked in pits of lime and water, and he had lifted it out and scraped off the fat and hairs. It had been softened in a pit full of manure and pigeon dung, and it had lain in pits containing solutions of tannin (an extract of crushed bark) that turned the hide into leather. The leather had been rinsed and dried in his shed, and finally he had rubbed and rubbed it with grease until it was as supple as woven cloth. All this, and the calfskin would now be cut into gloves for Walter Dragun and his friends.

DRYING SHED

OAK BARK

MANURE PITS

TANNING PITS

LIME PIT

DOG LICKING MEAT FROM A SKIN

SCRAPING AWAY THE HAIRS

Henry told his story to the leatherworkers and shoemakers who bought his tanned hides, but they only nodded in sympathy and carried on with their work.

The hides were treated differently for different purposes. Thick, stiff leather made saddles, horse collars, bridles, and straps, while shoe leather was soft for the uppers and hard for the soles. Some skins were supple enough to be quilted for the garments worn by knights under their armor. Other skins were stitched into purses for the merchants and their wives.

Thomas Savage was still in prison on Wednesday. Although Thomas's fiery temper often got him into trouble, he was an honest merchant who had never lodged thieves under his roof; but for some unknown reason, Walter Dragun had a grudge against him.

Thomas's house stood alongside Highgate, the main road running down to the bridge, south of the river, in the part of the town owned by the Abbot of Burg. Thomas's wife was being comforted by a sympathetic neighbor when the sound of pounding feet was heard coming up the street. The door suddenly burst open, and in stepped Walter Dragun, followed by Nicholas Pot, John Gerneys, and seven others. Pushing the women and children aside, they unhooked the fine brass pot from the fire, flung the midday stew all over the clean rushes, and swept two silver-rimmed wooden bowls from the shelf. Walter Dragun then climbed to the upper chamber, ransacked the chest, and pocketed two more of Thomas's silver bowls. Meanwhile, his men had slaughtered a sheep in the back garden, and they carried it away with the rest of the loot.

Thomas Savage was released the next day, but he was forced to pay good money for the return of his cooking pot and the bowls. Although he hotly resented the loss of the money, he was even more indignant at the way he had been molested in the marketplace and humiliated before all his friends.

Thomas's brass pots and silver bowls had been made in the metal-working shops that lined the narrow lanes between Broad Street and the High Street, and between the High Street and St. Mary's Street. Smiths heated the metals on charcoal fires and beat them into shape on their anvils, crafting fine pots and dishes for all of Stanford.

Sword blades wielded by great nobles such as Earl John de Warenne were imported from places like Cologne or Milan, but the ordinary freemen's sons probably got swords that were made in larger English towns and obtained through the agency of their local ironmongery (hardware) shop.

Leatherworkers made sword sheaths out of wood covered with leather and with fleecy linings, full of natural oil, to keep rust from the blades. Smiths made ornate daggers to hang from jeweled belts, bits for horses' bridles, stirrups for saddles, and spurs for noblemen's heels. Other metalworkers made gigantic shears for shearmen, scissors for tailors, keys for merchants' chests, and all kinds of objects, from tiny buckles to the great hooks and chains used down at the docks.

Stanford's annual fair gave all the town's craftsmen and merchants a chance to meet their foreign counterparts and do business to their mutual advantage. The fair was held during Lent. Easter of this year had fallen on April 22, and the two weeks before it had seen the streets and alleyways of the town crowded with strangers. Traders had come from all parts of Britain as well as distant lands overseas. The fair was controlled by Earl John de Warenne through his seneschal, Walter Dragun, who took a percentage of the profits. The merchants had to obey the earl's strict regulations. He commandeered all the shops and stalls in his part of town and rented them out to visiting merchants. It had always been the custom, under previous lords, to pay compensation to the shopkeepers. But ever since Earl John de Warenne and Walter Dragun had been in control of the fair, no compensation money had been paid out at all.

The earl did well out of the fair. Arguments were settled at his tribunal. Walter Dragun and his bailiffs inspected the quality of the goods and checked weights and measures. Tents and booths were set up in every corner, and money changers huddled over their tables as they counted the coins in the bitter spring wind. Mules and packhorses were tethered to every post, the stables were full, and the river was choked with boats and barges. Minstrels, jugglers, and tumblers ignored the austerities of Lent to amuse the crowds. Peddlers and tinkers did a roaring trade, while pickpockets and thieves made their own sharp living. Doctors and apothecaries sold their skills, performing on-the-spot surgery and handing out ointments and potions.

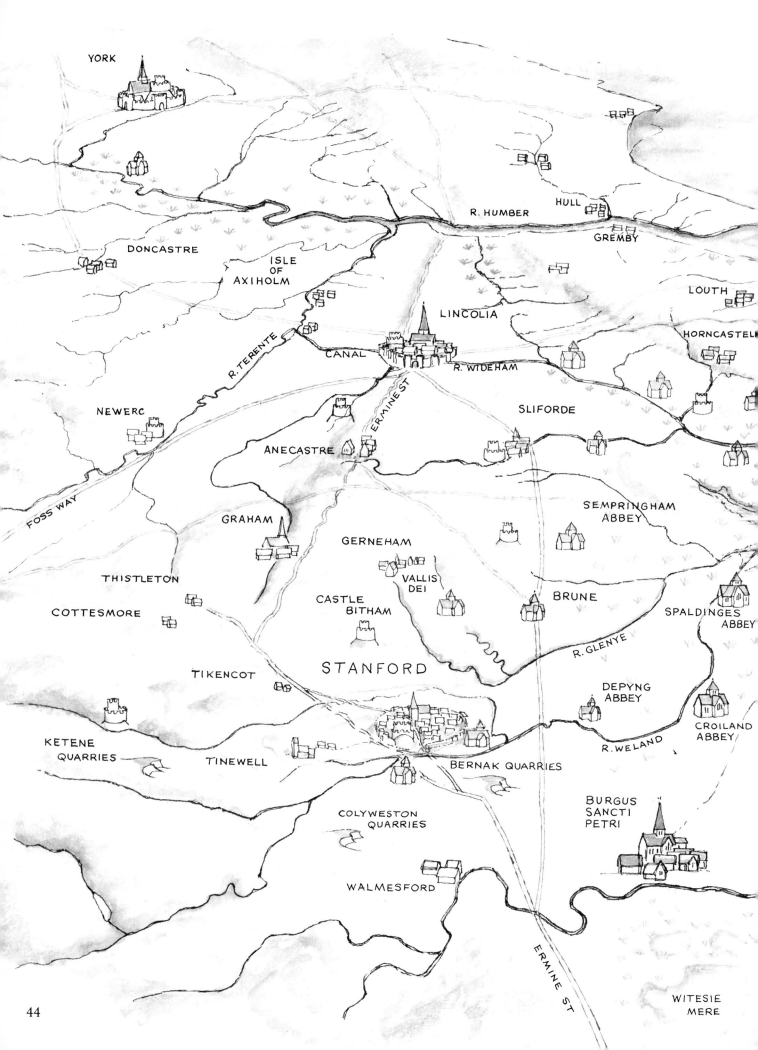

YORK

DONCASTRE

ISLE
OF
AXIHOLM

R. HUMBER

HULL

GREMBY

LOUTH

R. TERENTE

CANAL

LINCOLIA

HORNCASTEL

R. WIDEHAM

NEWERC

ERMINE ST

SLIFORDE

ANECASTRE

FOSS WAY

GRAHAM

GERNEHAM

SEMPRINGHAM
ABBEY

THISTLETON

VALLIS
DEI

BRUNE

SPALDINGES
ABBEY

COTTESMORE

CASTLE
BITHAM

R. GLENYE

STANFORD

DEPYNG
ABBEY

TIKENCOT

CROILAND
ABBEY

KETENE
QUARRIES

TINEWELL

BERNAK QUARRIES

R. WELAND

BURGUS
SANCTI
PETRI

COLYWESTON
QUARRIES

WALMESFORD

ERMINE ST

WITESIE
MERE

Most foreign merchants who came to Stanford for wool and other products attended the annual fair. There they hoped to display their own goods and make advantageous trades.

The Florentine merchant Fulk Clarissimus, however, had chosen to visit Stanford in August instead, because he could then travel on to summer fairs held in other parts of the country. He also said it was dangerous to cross the North sea in rough wintry weather, and even now he had prudently insured his precious cargoes against shipwreck and robbers with a banking firm before setting out. It had been a long, expensive journey, paying the river tolls up the Rhine and then crossing from Rotterdam to Botolfston. On Monday the goods had been unloaded from the large seagoing vessel to flat-bottomed river craft rented from the Abbot of Spaldinges. It would take three days for the Florentine cargoes to be rowed, towed, and punted up the River Weland to Stanford, but Fulk Clarissimus and his partner were covering the distance more rapidly on hired horses.

OLINGBROC CASTLE

BOTOLFSTON

THE WASSE

LENN

WISEBEC

R. OUSE

THORNEHAWE ABBEY

R. NEEN

ABBEYS

CASTLES

QUARRIES

At noon on Wednesday, all the notable merchants of Stanford were assembled in a large upper room opposite All Saints' Church, overlooking the market, waiting to greet their influential foreign guests. Tables were laid for a feast, and apprentice boys stood by with bowls of scented water for the travelers to wash their hands with before the meal. When Fulk Clarissimus was finally announced, he was closely followed by his young partner, Hugelin Sampe, and by the Florentine agent who lived permanently in Stanford and acted as interpreter. Florence was one of the greatest cities in the world, and its merchants often lived like nobles in marble palaces. Hugelin stared up at the rickety timber posts supporting the roof beams of the merchants' hall and thought wistfully of the magnificent buildings at home.

Fulk Clarissimus and Hugelin Sampe lodged at The Angel, St. Mary's Street, overlooking the bridge. There were not many inns in Stanford, because the king and nobility usually stayed with the friars or at St. Leonard's Priory when traveling up the Great North Road, while noble ladies lodged with the nuns of St. Michael. Any friend of Earl John de Warenne brought his noisy household and men-at-arms into the castle. The merchants, however, liked to be in the center of town, where they could meet their friends and talk business. They preferred the independence and good cheer of an inn to being stranded outside the walls with the monks.

The innkeeper of The Angel sold his own home-brewed ale and paid a tax twice a year to Earl John de Warenne, whose checkerboard emblem was painted on the doorpost.

The inn servants led Fulk's and Hugelin's horses to a stable at the back of the yard. There were several beds in the inn's upper chamber, and the Florentine merchants shared the accommodation with other travelers. People often slept two or three in a bed, even with strangers. There were fleas in the sheets, and rats and mice on the floor, but no one complained. What could be done against such small vermin?

ST MARY'S CHURCH

Thursday morning the first of the barges was moored to the timber wharf, while the other two were still being towed and punted against the current. Cranes hoisted the huge bales of silks and other goods up to carts standing on the quay, under the watchful eyes of Fulk Clarissimus and Hugelin Sampe. The Florentine agent was waiting to accompany the carts up the road and then to see the bales safely stored in the cellar under his house. At Eastbythewater on the far side of the river there were larger cranes, operated by men walking inside treadwheels, and these were unloading pine poles from Norway to be used as scaffolding around the tower of St. Mary's Church.

Later that morning Fulk Clarissimus was in his agent's house displaying a choice selection of his silks to Walter the Fleming. Walter's wife and daughter had begged to come along as well; they loved to look at the rare and beautiful fabrics, which were far too fine and expensive for them to hope to wear. The best of Fulk's woven silks would be made into magnificent church vestments; but some of them, with their delightful patterns of swans, fountains, hunting dogs, plants, and peacocks, would be cut and stitched into gowns and bought by court ladies. These sophisticated women would tuck the folds of a plain outer garment under an elbow, or into the belt, to show off the rich cloth of the undergarment. Fulk had dressed Walter's daughter in such a gown, but Walter was too busy to notice. He was taking a close look at a new material called velvet, where the looped weave had been clipped by the shearmen until it stood up like a miniature carpet. If Walter took such velvets to St. Bartholomew's Fair in London, he could make a fine profit.

Traders must make a profit, and that same day there was also hard bargaining between Fulk and Hugh, son of Walter of Tikencot. They inspected the soft white fleeces in Hugh's woolsacks stacked in his cellar. The Florentine agent translated, and Hugelin Sampe did his best to pick up a few English words. Hugh was satisfied with the price Fulk offered for ten of his large woolsacks, and the deal was concluded. Then Hugh brought out all the rolls of cloth so carefully woven by Godfrey of Reynham and his journeymen and so expertly fulled and tented by Walter the Fleming's workers. Fulk noted the evenness of the weave, and Hugelin exclaimed at the fine quality of the spun yarn. They admired the patterned materials: the striped and checkered cloth, and the twills where the shuttles had passed over one or two threads of weft at a time. They even liked the good plain tabby made by the apprentices. Fulk and Hugelin consulted together and bought the whole stock. Everyone was delighted. Business over, the two Florentine merchants visited all the shops in St. Mary's Hill, buying presents from Stanford to take home to their families and friends.

The Florentine visitors left at sunrise on Friday. The river ran high and fast under its banks as Fulk Clarissimus and Hugelin Sampe watched their bales of cloth, woolsacks, and other purchases safely loaded on the boats. Sails were hoisted, and the wind and current swept the three barges out of sight down the River Weland. With their servants and a local guide, the two men mounted their hired horses and trotted down the towpath. Walter the Fleming and Hugh, son of Walter of Tikencot, congratulated each other on the success of their sales and went straight to the money changer's table to transfer Italian coins and bills of exchange into silver pennies. Reginald the Dyer watched the business transactions with his usual keen interest.

Walter Dragun, the seneschal, and Hugh Bunting, the bailiff, stood apart on the quay calculating the money they had taken in tronage. The tron was the official weighing machine, and tronage was the tax due to the lord of Stanford on the export of goods. All the merchants said it was an unlawful tax and threatened to complain to the king, but the seneschal replied he was not afraid of the king, or anyone else for that matter. He obeyed only one man, Earl John de Warenne.

Trade flourished every time foreign merchants came to the town, whether from Scandinavia, the Low Countries, France, Germany, Spain, or Italy. As soon as the Florentines had left, money and goods began to change hands. Hugh, son of Walter of Tikencot, met Godfrey of Reynham outside All Saints' Church and gave him the balance due on the cloth he had sold to Fulk Clarissimus. Most of the money was needed for rent, but Godfrey gave a small purse to Alice, his wife, and she bought fine linen for a new veil. He gave another purse to Agnes of Tinewell for a new supply of spun yarn. Agnes bought new shoes and the shoemaker put the coins in a bag with the rest of his takings to buy a new hide from the tanner, Henry of Cottesmore.

Both Reginald the Dyer and Walter the Fleming were pleased to see so much activity in the marketplace next Monday. Reginald bought a new bridle for his horse, and Walter was measured for a new robe. The friars frowned and preached against the vanities of town life, but not many people were willing to listen. As usual, the bailiffs inspected the goods in the stalls, and Nicholas Pot was delighted to find faulty threads in a roll of twill. Walter Dragun happened to be passing on his tall, black horse and enjoyed extracting a particularly heavy fine.

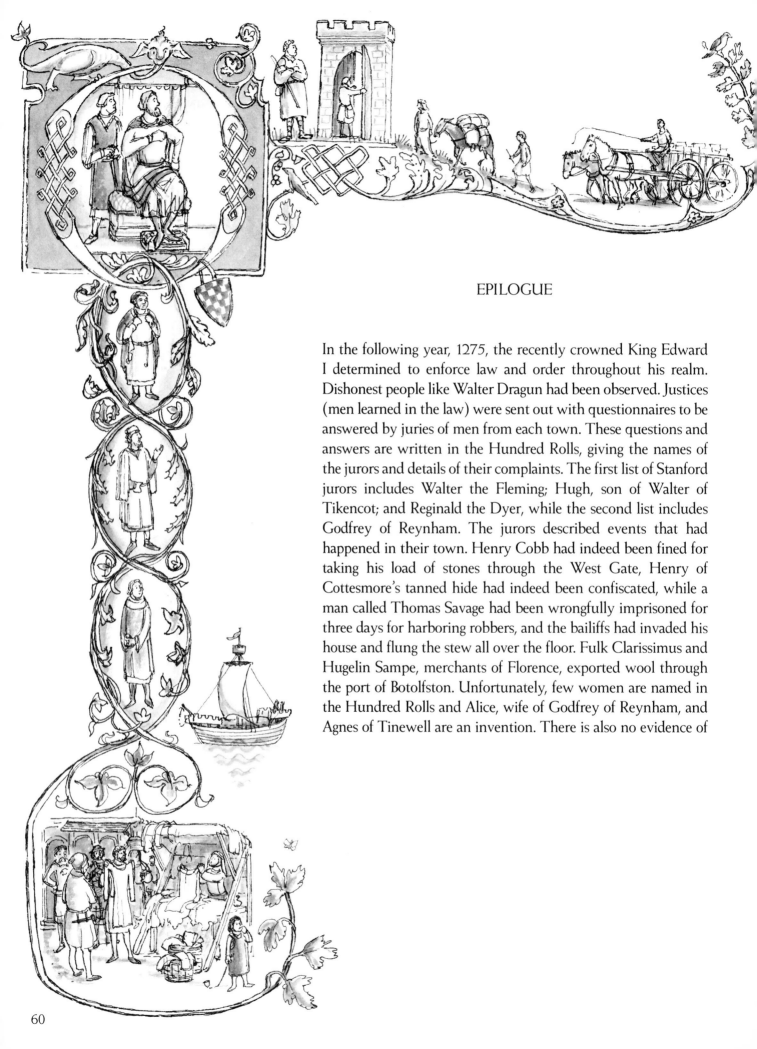

EPILOGUE

In the following year, 1275, the recently crowned King Edward I determined to enforce law and order throughout his realm. Dishonest people like Walter Dragun had been observed. Justices (men learned in the law) were sent out with questionnaires to be answered by juries of men from each town. These questions and answers are written in the Hundred Rolls, giving the names of the jurors and details of their complaints. The first list of Stanford jurors includes Walter the Fleming; Hugh, son of Walter of Tikencot; and Reginald the Dyer, while the second list includes Godfrey of Reynham. The jurors described events that had happened in their town. Henry Cobb had indeed been fined for taking his load of stones through the West Gate, Henry of Cottesmore's tanned hide had indeed been confiscated, while a man called Thomas Savage had been wrongfully imprisoned for three days for harboring robbers, and the bailiffs had invaded his house and flung the stew all over the floor. Fulk Clarissimus and Hugelin Sampe, merchants of Florence, exported wool through the port of Botolfston. Unfortunately, few women are named in the Hundred Rolls and Alice, wife of Godfrey of Reynham, and Agnes of Tinewell are an invention. There is also no evidence of

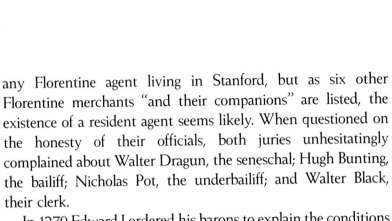

any Florentine agent living in Stanford, but as six other Florentine merchants "and their companions" are listed, the existence of a resident agent seems likely. When questioned on the honesty of their officials, both juries unhesitatingly complained about Walter Dragun, the seneschal; Hugh Bunting, the bailiff; Nicholas Pot, the underbailiff; and Walter Black, their clerk.

In 1279 Edward I ordered his barons to explain the conditions under which they came to own their estates. The fourteenth-century chronicler Hemingburgh described how hotly Earl John de Warenne resented the question. "When asked by what warranty he held his franchises . . . he lost his temper, produced an ancient rusty sword and exclaimed, 'Here is my warranty. My ancestors, who came with William the Bastard [William the Conqueror], conquered their lands with the sword, and with the sword I will defend them against all who desire to seize them. For the king did not conquer his lands by himself, but our ancestors were his partners and helpers.'" In 1281 Earl John de Warenne was deprived of his most important administrative privileges, but nothing is known of the fate of Walter Dragun and his bailiffs. Their names disappear from the records.

THE NAMES

Our language has taken thousands of years to evolve, and place-names have developed along similar lines. Some places have received relatively modern names, while others can be traced right back to the original inhabitants of the British Isles.

The Celts had words to describe hills, rivers, forests, and other natural features, and many Celtic names survive to this day. Then came the Romans to bestow Latin names on their camps, towns, and settlements. At the turn of the fifth century the Saxon invaders used a totally different form of speech and laid the foundation of modern English. Another rich vocabulary was introduced by the Danes in the ninth century, and they founded the villages in the Stanford area. The last significant tide of foreign words swept in with the Norman invasion of 1066. Norman French was still spoken at court in 1274, the year of *Walter Dragun's Town*, but there are few Norman place names in Walter's part of the country.

The use of surnames, in the modern sense, did not become general in England until the thirteenth and fourteenth centuries. Before then, people used their Christian names, which were sometimes so popular that a descriptive name had to be added for identification. A man was often described as being the son of his father, or the inhabitant of a certain place—the name of Hugh, son of Walter of Tikencot, does both. Other names described a man's trade, his character, or appearance. When a man's own personal name was passed on to a son or grandson, who may have had none of his characteristics, it became a surname. Women were usually called "daughter of" or "wife of" the father or husband.

Origins of place-names mentioned in the text

Botolfston BOSTON Saint Botulf's stone. The saint may have preached from a stone or cross at this place.

Burg PETERBOROUGH Originally called Medeshamstede, the homestead of Mede. Houses and an abbey were built, but when the monks' quarters were destroyed by the Danes, the place was simply called Burg, meaning town. With the building of the new abbey dedicated to St. Peter, the town became known as Burgus Sancti Petri.

Cottesmore A cot, or cottage, on a moor.

Gerneham IRNHAM Georna was a Saxon leader, and "ham" was a Saxon word for a homestead or village.

Lenn KING'S LYNN This was probably the Celtic "llyn," for lake, describing the pool at the rivermouth. Lenn only became King's Lynn in the sixteenth century, when the town received a royal charter.

Spaldinges SPALDING Place-names ending with "ing" date back to the earliest Saxon times, meaning "the people of." In this case the people of the Spaldas tribe.

Stanford STAMFORD Sometimes spelled Steanford, the name meant a stone ford.

Tikencot TICKENCOTE "Ticcen" was the Saxon word for a kid (young goat), and although "cote" usually stood for a cottage, it could also mean an animal shelter. Saxons may have raised goats here.

Tinewell TINWELL "Well" indicated a well, stream, or spring. In this case it meant "the stream of Tida's people."

Weland WELLAND This Celtic river name probably meant "good river."

Origins of surnames mentioned in the text

Black, Walter. A name usually given to men with black hair or dark complexions.

Bunting, Hugh. "Bunting" was a word of affection usually reserved for little children, as with "Bye, baby bunting," derived from "bon," meaning "good." But Hugh Bunting was a nasty fellow, and this is surely an example of medieval sarcasm.

Cobb, Henry. "Cobb" was short for Jacob.

Dragun, Walter. Medieval dragons were fire-breathing serpentlike creatures with sharp claws, scaly skins, and fierce tempers. He must have been heartily disliked to have earned such a name.

Fleming, Walter the. One of Walter's forebears came from Flanders.

Gerneys, John. "Guernon" meant "mustache" and perhaps his was a particularly fine one.

Luterel, Sir Robert. "Loutre" was French for "otter," and a member of the family was called "le Lutrer," or "otter hunter."

Pot, Nicholas. "Pot," short for Philipot, and derived from Philip.

Reynham, Godfrey of. His native settlement may have vanished. There is no Reynham Village in the Stanford area.

Savage, Thomas. Someone with a wild, fierce temper.

Tikencot, Hugh, son of Walter of. At least some members of this large and prosperous family would have lived at the nearby village of Tikencote.

Warenne, Earl John de. Named after the family estate of Varenne in Normandy.

Abbey (28, 44–45) A community of monks or nuns governed by an abbot or abbess. Abbey is also used to describe the buildings in which they lived.

Bailey (18–19) A courtyard. The area of ground enclosed by the castle wall and related buildings. Some castles had two or more baileys, but Stanford only had one.

Bailiff (17–18) Bailiffs and underbailiffs were the officials who carried out the orders of the seneschal, making arrests, extracting fines, and generally looking after the interests of their employer— in this case Earl John de Warenne. (A bailiff could also be one of the king's officers, or an officer in some other important position, but that was another use of the word.)

Bill of exchange (56) A document arranging for the transfer of money, similar to a modern-day check.

Carding (11) A system of brushing wool between two wooden boards, fitted with prickly teasel heads or wires, to prepare it for spinning. The process removed dirt and brushed the fibers into the same direction. Then the wool was rolled off the cards in a tube, trapping air and adding warmth to the finished yarn.

Cathedral city (32) A city with a cathedral and resident bishop. A cathedral was the bishop's own church, and he administered his diocese from his neighboring palace.

Chancel (27) The eastern part of a church, held sacred and reserved for the use of the clergy.

Combing (11) A process of preparing long strands of wool for spinning. The wool was placed in the teeth of an iron comb that had been firmly fixed to a post. Another comb was then swung against it to comb out the dirt and tangles until the fibers hung down in parallel strands. Combs worked better if they were oiled and heated.

Conduit (5) The correct name for this little building is conduit head, but the last word is often left out. The word conduit is used to describe a channel carrying water from one place to another. In medieval times conduits were made of hollowed-out tree trunks or, occasionally, lead piping. Water would be carried from a spring in the hills (sometimes covered by an "intake house") to a cistern inside the conduit head, where it was available whenever anyone pulled up the pegs in the spouts.

Constable (18) The official in command of a castle.

Distaff (11) A wooden stick, often forked at the top. The combed or carded wool was wound and tied to the top of the distaff, which was then tucked under the arm, or into the belt, leaving the left hand free to draw out the fibers (see spinning).

Dorter (31) A dormitory. A large room where the monks or nuns slept.

Freemen (40) A class of men who enjoyed personal freedom and were able to travel about, unlike the peasants, who were "tied to the land" and thus compelled to live their lives in the place where they were born.

Fulling (23) A process that thickened the cloth and closed up the tiny holes in the weave in order to make it wind- and waterproof. Workers got into troughs or tubs of water and trampled the woven cloth with their bare feet. When fuller's earth (23), a substance similar to clay, was added to the water, it helped to remove the oil and grease. This laborious job was mechanized at an early date by the use of fulling mills (23). These worked on the same system as the water mills used for grinding corn: Huge hammers rose and fell as the wheels revolved, beating and turning the cloth in wooden troughs.

Gatehouse (18) Literally, a house over a gate. A castle gatehouse was usually built as a tower, with a portcullis chamber over the entrance passage and guardrooms on either side. The gatehouse was used to defend the entrance to the castle.

Hundred (3) In Saxon and Danish times the area around Stanford was divided into districts called Wappentakes or Hundreds. These names were still in use in the thirteenth century when the king circulated his questionnaire to find out what conditions were like in each district. The questions and answers were written on parchment scrolls called the Hundred Rolls. The word "hundred" referred to a district, not a number.

Keep (19) The strongest building in a castle. A besieged garrison could rush into the keep and continue to defend itself after the rest of the castle had fallen to the enemy.

Matins (31) The first of the series of "canonical hours," or set of prayers, undertaken by monks and nuns. Matins took place at a time between midnight and 2:00 A.M. and lasted for up to two hours, after which came another service called lauds.

Monastery (28) This word described only the building or buildings in which the monks or nuns lived and not the actual community of monks or nuns. (Nowadays it usually applies only to buildings inhabited by monks.)

Nave (27) The main body of a church, lying west of the chancel, often flanked by aisles, and used by the congregation. Pews were not introduced until late medieval times.

Parish (26) A district of a town or country. England was split up into parishes well before the Norman Conquest in 1066, and each parish had its own church and priest. The priest looked after the spiritual welfare of the inhabitants while they, in turn, kept the church in repair and paid tithes, supplying the priest with food, drink, and other needs.

Peddler (43) A trader in small goods such as ribbons, belts, trinkets, etc.

Priory (28) A religious house where the monks or nuns were governed by a prior or prioress. A priory was often the offshoot of an abbey, and less important.

Sacristan (31) The person in charge of the interior of a church, who looked after its treasures, vestments, etc. A sacristan supplied the candles, replenished the oil in the lamps, and rang the bells.

Selvage (or selvedge) (23) The firm edges running along the two sides of a length of woven cloth.

Seneschal (16) Kings and great nobles employed seneschals to run their estates in the same way as stewards acted as overseers in the manors. A seneschal made judgments in his lord's court, saw justice was carried out, and commanded all the domestic arrangements of the castle.

Shuttle (8) A hollow, boat-shaped tool, pointed at both ends, carrying thread that was wound around a little bobbin. The bobbin turned in its socket and the thread unwound as the shuttle was cast across the loom.

Smith (40) A craftsman working in iron or other metals.

Spinning (9) The process of converting wool into yarn. In these early days the fibers of wool were drawn from the top of the distaff with the fingers of one hand, while the other twisted and rotated the spindle. The spindle was a little stick, notched at the top to hold the yarn, and thrust through a hole in a whorl. The whorl was a stone or clay weight that acted as a flywheel, adding momentum to the spin. When the spinner had finished a length of yarn, she wound it around the spindle.

Tanner (35) A man who converted raw hides, or skins, into leather. After many laborious processes the tanner would steep the hides in a succession of pits containing solutions of tannin. In medieval times tannin was usually extracted from oak bark, and it had the useful properties of preserving the hide and making it waterproof.

Tenting (23) Cloth came out of the fulling troughs wet and considerably shrunk. Although it never regained its original length and width, the tenting operation stretched it back into shape as it dried in the open air. Tenting frames were basically long lines of rails, set up like fences. One selvage edge of the cloth was held on little hooks running along the top rail and the other caught by hooks at the bottom (origin of the expression "on tenterhooks"). The cloth was held taut between the two.

Tinker (43) One who mended broken pots and pans.

Vestments (53) Special clothes worn by the clergy for church services.

Warp (8) Parallel threads running the length of the loom. The threads were wound around the warp beam at the back of the loom, which could be rotated by means of a stick close to the weaver's hand. Toward the other end of the loom, the threads passed through loops in the healds, which were sets of cords suspended between pairs of bars. Foot pedals were tied to the healds with cords, and the weaver could raise and lower alternate threads with his feet, creating a shed, or space, through which the shuttle was cast. The finished cloth was wound around a cloth beam by the weaver's seat.

Weft (8) Thread from the shuttle, woven across the loom at right angles to the warp.

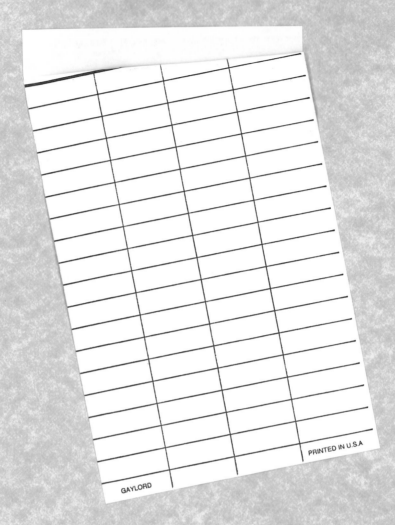

GAYLORD

PRINTED IN U.S.A